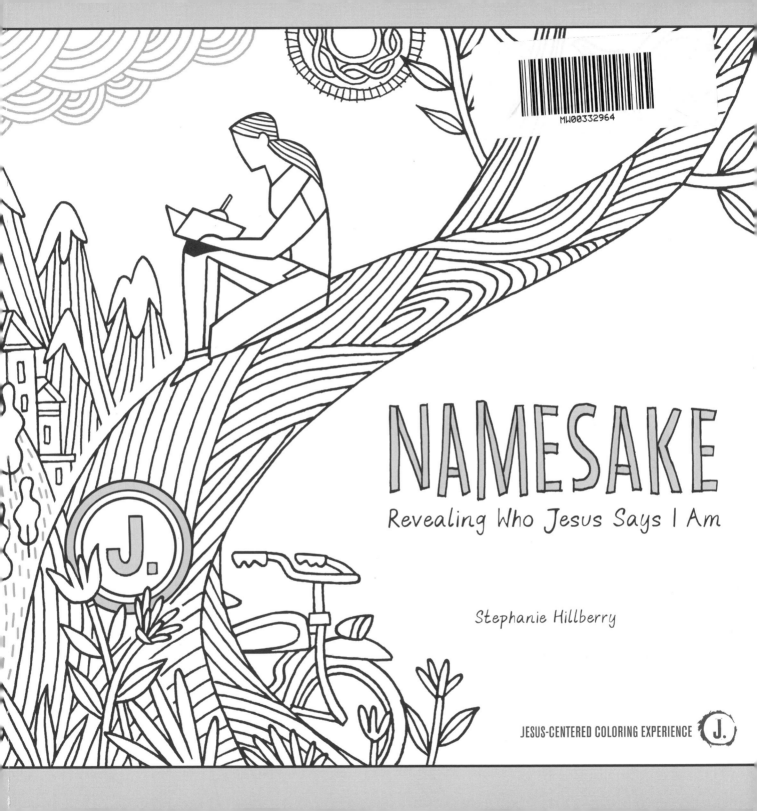

NAMESAKE

Revealing Who Jesus Says I Am

Stephanie Hillberry

JESUS-CENTERED COLORING EXPERIENCE   J.

Jesus-Centered Coloring Experience
NAMESAKE
Revealing Who Jesus Says I Am

Copyright © 2017 Group Publishing, Inc.
group.com

Credits
Author: Stephanie Hillberry
Chief Creative Officer: Joani Schultz
Senior Editor: Candace McMahan
Art Director: Michael Paustian
Illustrator: Matt Wood
Production Artist: Veronica Preston
Cover Art: Matt Wood
Production Manager: Melissa Towers

ISBN 978-1-4707-4277-5
10 9 8 7 6 5 4 3 2 1   26 25 24 23 22 21 20 19 18 17
Printed in the U.S.A.

JESUS HAS GIVEN YOU HIS NAME

It's time to pause, relax, breathe, and rest a little.

It's time to empty your mind of racing thoughts, worries, and a never-ending to-do list and to fill your heart and your mind with color and creativity and peace.

While you're doing this, it's also time to ask Jesus one of the most important questions you'll ever ask:

"Jesus, who do you say I am?"

Then listen for his response. With each new stroke of color, listen to him speak to you about who he's created you to be. New. Growing. Free. Friend.

With each new page, you'll find a new perspective on your identity in Jesus. Let this identity sink in as you color and reflect. The process will leave you with a vibrant work of art...

...and something far more valuable: his namesake.

You're Becoming

NEW

It gets old being the old you, doesn't it?

Stuck in patterns, letting others down,

rinse and repeat.

Here's what I offer instead:

a new you with new patterns.

My patterns.

I promise they'll never get old.

Inspired by 2 Corinthians 5:17

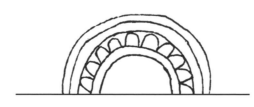

You're MY Work

You're so busy working
that it's easy to think
I'm one more thing to do.
But I do not need your works.
Instead, you're my work,
and I love my work.
Let's labor together for love
and sacrifice and the good fight.

Inspired by Ephesians 2:10

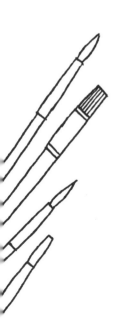

You're
CHOSEN

For all the lonely times you were left out,

passed over, left behind,

I have this to say:

You're chosen by me,

picked and set aside.

You're now my insider,

bearing my mark,

never alone again.

Inspired by Colossians 3:12

You're

GROWING

When you're feeling dried up and brittle,

remember who you are connected to,

and stop trying to pull your own nourishment

up from the ground.

Put away your brittle self,

and see the truth:

As part of *my* root system,

you are healthy, verdant, and growing.

Inspired by John 15:1, 5

You're in a

SPACIOUS

Place

Rules are bullies.

They push you around,

cramming you into a mold

that looks good on the outside

but squeezes your heart.

My way is different.

It's a mold that fits you perfectly;

open, spacious, *right.*

Inspired by Romans 8:2

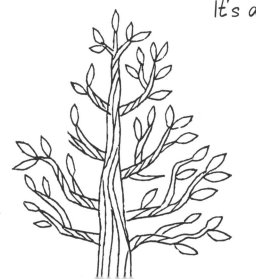

You're
OVERFLOWING

Left alone, you'll always come up short.

Short on time, on discipline, on patience.

But when you come up short,

that's when I begin.

So quit believing that you're empty.

I'm overflowing,

and there's plenty to go around.

Inspired by Ephesians 1:3

You're

CONFIDENT

I can see you holding back,

timidly hiding your thoughts and emotions from me.

I have not asked you to do this – to edit and censor yourself.

I want you to be confident,

to be bold, to be brash.

Take the risk of being yourself.

Inspired by Ephesians 3:12

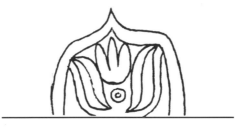

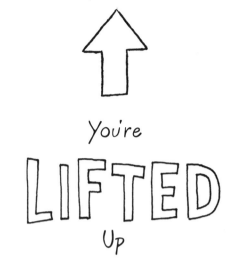

You're
LIFTED
Up

When the muck of life
starts pulling you down like quicksand,
I will rescue you.
I will lift you up to where I live,
above the mire where the air is clean
and the breeze is fresh.

Inspired by Ephesians 2:6

You're My Crack of

LIGHT

Some people are completely closed to me.

But not you.

You're open.

You hope,

you wait,

you believe against reason.

You're my crack of light

in a closed world.

Inspired by 2 Corinthians 3:14

You're

FREE

That sneering, critical voice in your head
is a false warden holding you captive,
counting on your compliance.
But haven't you heard?
I've set you free.
You can walk right out of that cell
you've put yourself in.
Just open the door.

Inspired by Romans 8:1

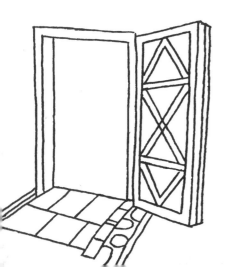

You're my

FRIEND

As your friend, I'm for you.
I don't tell your secrets.
I don't leave you out.
I'm not friends with you
because I have to be
but because I picked you.
That's what friends do.

Inspired by John 15:15

You
DESTROY
Darkness

That fiend darkness,

swallowing hope and extinguishing faith.

It seems impenetrable, unstoppable.

But not against you.

You're a bright, blazing destroyer of darkness,

crushing it with my light.

Inspired by Matthew 5:14

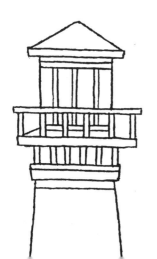

You're a

VICTOR

Sometimes it feels like you're losing the battle.

Losing to cancer, to failure.

Losing to love gone sour.

But hold on.

I have a secret:

The game is rigged.

Losing is winning when

I set the rules, and I've already won this game.

Inspired by Romans 8:37

You're

WEAK

(And That's Okay)

All this work you're putting
into getting it all together isn't working.
No matter what you do,
you're still fragile and flawed
and sinful and selfish.
So quit trying so hard,
and be weak instead.
Let me be the strong one.
I'm better at it.

Inspired by 2 Corinthians 12:7-9

You Have My
SPIRIT

Your experience of being mortal – living in your body,
dwelling on Earth – is a shadow of what's true.

My Spirit is the full truth.

It's more spirit than flesh,

more heaven than Earth,

more eternal than temporal.

And it's growing stronger in you every day.

Inspired by John 3:3-6

You Receive My

GRACE

I know you'd like to help — that you'd feel better
if you could chip in, or work it off,
or carry some of your own weight.
Sorry. I've got it covered.
My grace is a gift,
and there's nothing you can do to earn it.
Just receive it with a thankful heart.

Inspired by Ephesians 2:8

You're

WISE

When Others Are Foolish

You have wisdom that's not from this world.
You give when you should keep,
serve when you should lead,
surrender when you should fight.
I cherish this wisdom because it comes from me.
It is the true path that exposes foolishness
masquerading as good sense.

Inspired by 1 Corinthians 1:30

You Make Spaces

SACRED

My Spirit within you cannot be contained.
You bring my presence with you wherever you go,
turning mundane places into sacred spaces.
I do not need your invitation
or permission to come –
you've already brought me here.

Inspired by 1 Corinthians 6:19

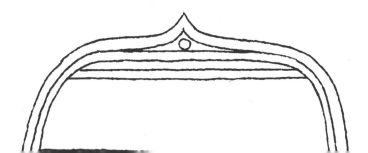

You're

WITH

Me

Don't waste your time on comparisons.
Whether you're better or worse
or different or the same,
it doesn't matter.
There are no outsiders – there's just me
and those who are with me.
We are one spirit and one group,
including you.

Inspired by Galatians 3:28

You're

FORGIVEN

There will be times you let me down.

Times you let down the people you love.

Times you hurt, wound, afflict, offend.

But for each of these times,

I heal, restore, redeem, and forgive.

My grace covers your sin,

and it is more than enough.

Inspired by Ephesians 1:7

You Have

EVERYTHING

You Need

Your true needs are not what you think.

You want smooth, happy, plenty.

But I know that bumpy, weak, and lacking are better for you

because they are my refiner's fire.

I'll choose your holiness over your happiness every time,

for it is precious to me.

Inspired by Philippians 4:19

SAFETY

You're

PROTECTED

It's difficult to understand why
I expose you to pain – why I do not intervene.
But here's what you don't see:
I'm always guarding your heart and your mind, and *nothing* –
not even death – can climb over my wall of protection
to steal your joy and peace.

Inspired by Philippians 4:7

PEACE

You're a

KINGDOM

Bearer

My kingdom is different from the ones you're used to.

It embraces instead of divides,

serves instead of promotes,

forgives instead of harms.

And because I'm in you,

you're bringing my kingdom to the *here* and *now*.

Let it expand and influence,

converting darkness into light.

Inspired by Philippians 3:20

You're My

HEIR

You're heir to the King and all the riches of his kingdom.
Heirs do not inherit by merit but by blood.
My blood.
You're also heir to something else you'd rather forget:
my suffering.
It doesn't make sense for to you to inherit such a thing,
but it offers a mysterious reward.

Inspired by Romans 8:17

You're

WELCOME

as You Are

You're welcome at my table just as you are.
You don't have to clean up, dress up, or shape up.
I ask that you receive others the same way,
just as they are.
Extend your heart to them
and begin to see them the way I do.

Inspired by Romans 15:7

You're

FRESH

Life

Bad words, attitudes, and ideas fill the air
like a pungent smell.
But then you enter,
and you're like the very essence of spring.
Like a natural purifier, your words bring life,
freshening those around you
like newly cut grass and crisp spring air.

Inspired by 2 Corinthians 2:14

You Will Not Be

MOVED

When you feel like your feet are slipping, remember this:

I will keep you grounded.

I'm standing behind you, holding you up.

I'm at your feet, pressing your soles to the ground.

You will not be moved.

Inspired by Ephesians 3:17

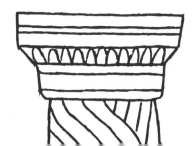

You're

HIDDEN

Away

You should know that I'm not the sharing type.
Now that you're mine, I'm hiding you away,
beyond the reach of the enemy's supernatural powers.
Though he covets you for his purposes,
you've been set aside for *my* purpose,
and my hiding place is secure.

Inspired by Colossians 3:3

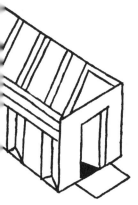

You Bring Out the

BEST

Though the world is full of robust flavors,
they leave an artificial aftertaste on the tongue.
But *not you.*
You're salt.
Natural and authentic,
you bring out the best flavors
in those around you.
You're my preserving agent,
unlocking the true taste of the life you've found in me.

Inspired by Matthew 5:13

You're Focused on What Matters

Your thoughts frequently buzz around

like frenzied bees in a hive.

Some offer a sweet nectar,

but others offend with a sting.

If you'll let me, I can transform this frenzy

into a calm, harmonized hum

by directing each thought toward one focal point:

Me.

Inspired by Hebrews 3:1

You're a

CHILD

Again

Through me, you have become a child of God.
How long has it been since you've been given permission
to be a kid - to play without restraint
and create without obligation?
Let me worry your worries
and take on your responsibilities.
Let me release you from adulthood
to be a child again.

Inspired by John 1:12

Your

LIFE

Is Mine

"Busy."

"A work in progress."

"All right."

You often describe your life with words like these.

But I have a new description of you: Me.

It seems like a strange way to describe your life,

but after you said yes to my salvation,

your life was traded for mine.

Now I'm the word that matters most.

Inspired by Colossians 3:4

You're

MY

Messenger

You're my messenger to a lost and hurting world.
Don't be so busy or distracted that you speak rashly;
instead, let me speak life through you.
Speak it boldly, speak it often.
And believe that speaking it will accomplish my purpose.

Inspired by 1 Thessalonians 2:4

You're

RESISTANT

(In a Good Way)

I'm proud that you don't make a habit of sinning.

You avoid temptation;

you don't linger in bad places;

you withhold judgment and sharp words.

This resistance is challenging,

but I'm by your side, helping you triumph.

Inspired by 1 John 5:18

You're on the

RIGHT

Track

I'm cheering for you.

Those things in your heart - I care about them, too.

That vision you see - pursue it.

Those obstacles you encounter - persevere.

Nothing can stand in your way when I'm for you.

Inspired by Romans 8:31-32

You're

TRUSTING

It's audacious to trust in someone you can't see or touch,
but you do it anyway.
Every day you entrust your life – your eternity – to me.
I will prove to you again and again that I'm trustworthy,
and I welcome you into the great and marvelous risk
of taking me at my word.

Inspired by Galatians 2:20

You're

TRUTH

Here's the truth about truth:

It's not a moving target;

it's not popular opinion;

it's not majority wins.

I am Truth, and because I am in you,

you and the rest of my followers are also truth.

When you follow my example by loving, serving, and healing,

you're pillars of truth, stabilizing this world.

Inspired by 1 Timothy 3:15

You Keep Things

BETWEEN

Us

When you honor me
through your worship, generosity, and love,
you aren't trying to impress others.
I love this about you,
because it doesn't matter what others think.
Only my eyes matter,
and only your heart matters.
Let's keep things between us.

Inspired by Matthew 6:4, 8, 18

You're Outrageously

CAREFREE

Though it may not feel like it,
you're outrageously carefree.
Because I've provided for all your needs,
you have no need for worry.
Ever.
This carefree spirit seems careless to the world,
but don't let that diminish your levity.
Embrace the freedom I offer,
for it is an enviable gift.

Inspired by Matthew 6:26

You

PLEASE

Me

Though your natural way - your *old* way -
seeks approval from others.
I have set you free from their hold over you.
You were not meant to be a people-pleaser,
boxed into their expectations and whims.
You please me.
Period.
My approval is all you need.

Inspired by 1 Thessalonians 2:4

Where will Jesus interrupt you?

Dreaded chore...or a chance to slow down and pay attention to Jesus? When we invite Jesus to interrupt every moment of our lives—not just the quiet, tidy ones—suddenly even chores take on a whole new purpose.

For books, Bibles, devotions, planners, and coloring experiences that move Jesus into EVERY corner of your life, visit...

JesusCenteredLife.com

#JesusInterruption

LIFETRE